Guenther Steiner

Guenther Steiner is an Italian motorsport executive and the current team principal of the Haas Formula One Team. He was born on April 7, 1965, in Merano, Italy. Steiner has been involved in motorsport for several decades, having started his career as a mechanic in the 1980s. He went on to work for various teams in Formula One, including Jaguar Racing, Red Bull Racing, and the now-defunct Toyota Racing.

In 2014, Steiner joined the newly-formed Haas F1 Team as team principal. The team made its debut in the 2016 Formula One season and has since established itself as a mid-field contender. Steiner is known for his straight-talking style and has been praised for his leadership and management skills.

Prior to his current role, Steiner served as a technical director for the Jaguar Racing team from 2001 to 2003 and as a sporting director for the Red Bull Racing team from 2005 to 2007. He also worked as a consultant for the now-defunct Toyota Racing team in 2009.

Steiner's experience and expertise in motorsport have made him a respected figure in the industry. He has been instrumental in the development and success of the Haas F1 Team, which has become known for its innovative approach to racing.

Under Steiner's leadership, the Haas F1 Team has forged a close relationship with Ferrari, which provides the team with engines, transmission, and other technical support. This partnership has helped the team to achieve impressive results, including several top-ten finishes and two fifth-place finishes in the Constructors' Championship in 2018 and 2019.

Despite the team's success, Steiner has not been afraid to speak his mind when he feels that the sport is not being run in a fair and transparent manner. In 2020, he publicly criticized the handling of the Racing Point brake ducts controversy, which he felt unfairly penalized his team and others.

Overall, Guenther Steiner is a highly respected and experienced figure in the world of motorsport. His leadership has helped to establish the Haas F1 Team as a force to be reckoned with, and his willingness to speak his mind has made him a popular and respected figure among fans and colleagues alike.

In addition to his role as team principal of the Haas F1 Team, Steiner is also known for his involvement in the development of young drivers. He has played a key role in the Haas Driver Development Program, which aims to identify and nurture young driving talent.

Steiner's experience and expertise have also led to his involvement in various motorsport organizations. He is a member of the FIA Formula One Commission and has served on the board of directors of the Grand Prix Drivers' Association.

Outside of motorsport, Steiner is known for his love of skiing and has been involved in various ski-related businesses. He is also a co-owner of a vineyard in his native Italy.

Overall, Guenther Steiner is a highly respected and influential figure in the world of motorsport. His leadership, experience, and willingness to speak his mind have made him a popular and respected figure among fans, colleagues, and drivers alike.

Steiner is known for his straightforward approach to management and leadership, which has helped him to achieve success both on and off the track. He has been praised by drivers and colleagues for his ability to motivate and inspire his team, and his focus on teamwork and collaboration has been a key factor in the success of the Haas F1 Team.

Despite the challenges and setbacks that come with competing in Formula One, Steiner remains committed to the sport and to the development of his team. He has shown a willingness to adapt and evolve his approach, and is constantly looking for ways to improve and build on the team's success.

Looking to the future, Steiner and the Haas F1 Team face a number of challenges as they strive to remain competitive in a rapidly evolving sport. However, with Steiner's leadership and expertise, there is no doubt that the team will continue to make its mark in the world of Formula One racing.

In recent years, Steiner has also become known for his appearances in the Netflix documentary series "Drive to Survive", which offers an inside look at the world of Formula One racing. Steiner's frank and colorful commentary has made him a fan favorite on the show, and has helped to further elevate his profile in the sport.

Despite his high profile and success, Steiner remains humble and focused on the task at hand. He is deeply committed to the development of his team and to the sport of Formula One, and is widely respected for his passion, dedication, and expertise.

In conclusion, Guenther Steiner is a highly respected and influential figure in the world of motorsport. His leadership, expertise, and willingness to speak his mind have made him a popular and respected figure among fans, colleagues, and drivers alike, and his focus on teamwork and collaboration has been a key factor in the success of the Haas F1 Team. With Steiner at the helm, there is no doubt that the team will continue to make its mark in the world of Formula One racing.

Looking ahead, Steiner faces new challenges in his role as team principal of the Haas F1 Team. In 2021, the team made the difficult decision to focus on developing their car for the 2022 season, which has meant a significant reduction in performance for the current season. This decision was made with an eye to the future, as the team seeks to be competitive and successful in the long term.

Steiner has also expressed his commitment to nurturing and developing young driving talent, which he sees as a key part of the team's future success. The Haas Driver Development Program has already produced several talented young drivers, and Steiner is eager to continue this work in the coming years.

Despite the challenges that lie ahead, there is no doubt that Guenther Steiner will continue to be a driving force in the world of motorsport. His leadership, expertise, and commitment to excellence have made him a respected and influential figure in the sport, and his dedication to the development of young drivers bodes well for the future of the Haas F1 Team.

As the sport of Formula One continues to evolve and change, Steiner remains committed to adapting and staying ahead of the curve. He has shown a willingness to embrace new technologies and strategies, and is constantly looking for ways to improve and build on the team's success.

In addition to his work with the Haas F1 Team, Steiner is also involved in various motorsport organizations and initiatives. He has been an outspoken advocate for greater transparency and fairness in the sport, and has played a key role in shaping the future of Formula One.

Overall, Guenther Steiner is a highly respected and influential figure in the world of motorsport. His leadership, expertise, and commitment to excellence have made him a popular and respected figure among fans, colleagues, and drivers alike, and his focus on teamwork and collaboration has been a key factor in the success of the Haas F1 Team. With Steiner at the helm, there is no doubt that the team will continue to make its mark in the world of Formula One racing for many years to come.

Looking even further ahead, Steiner is likely to face new challenges and opportunities as the sport of Formula One continues to evolve. With new regulations and technologies on the horizon, there will be new opportunities for innovation and improvement, and Steiner's experience and expertise will be invaluable in navigating these changes.

One area that Steiner is particularly focused on is the development of sustainable and environmentally friendly technologies in Formula One. He has spoken out about the importance of reducing the sport's carbon footprint and promoting sustainable practices, and has been involved in various initiatives aimed at promoting sustainability in the sport.

Overall, Guenther Steiner's contributions to the world of motorsport have been significant and far-reaching. His leadership, expertise, and commitment to excellence have made him a respected and influential figure in the sport, and his focus on teamwork and collaboration has been a key factor in the success of the Haas F1 Team. As the sport continues to evolve and change, Steiner's experience and expertise will undoubtedly be invaluable in shaping the future of Formula One racing.

In addition to his work in Formula One, Steiner has also been involved in other areas of motorsport. He has served as a team principal in various other racing series, including the American Le Mans Series, the FIA World Endurance Championship, and the Deutsche Tourenwagen Masters.

Steiner's experience in these other racing series has given him a unique perspective on the world of motorsport, and has helped him to develop a wide range of skills and expertise. He has also been involved in various driver development programs, helping to nurture and develop young driving talent in a range of different racing disciplines.

Looking to the future, Steiner's expertise and experience will undoubtedly be valuable in shaping the direction of motorsport as a whole. With his focus on teamwork, collaboration, and sustainable practices, he is well-positioned to help guide the sport towards a more positive and sustainable future.

Overall, Guenther Steiner is a highly respected and influential figure in the world of motorsport. His leadership, expertise, and commitment to excellence have made him a popular and respected figure among fans, colleagues, and drivers alike, and his focus on teamwork and collaboration has been a key factor in the success of the Haas F1 Team. With Steiner at the helm, there is no doubt that the team will continue to make its mark in the world of Formula One racing, and that his contributions to the sport as a whole will be felt for many years to come.

Career
Rally (1986–2001)

Guenther Steiner began his career in motorsport as a rally driver in 1986. He competed in a variety of national and international rally events, including the European Rally Championship and the World Rally Championship.

Steiner achieved a number of notable successes during his rallying career, including a second-place finish in the 1996 European Rally Championship and a podium finish in the 1998 Rally Australia.

Steiner continued to compete in rallying until 2001, when he retired from competitive driving to focus on other aspects of motorsport. However, his experience and expertise in rally racing would prove to be valuable assets in his future roles as a team manager and racing executive.

After retiring from competitive driving, Guenther Steiner shifted his focus to team management and executive roles in motorsport. He worked as a team manager for the Maserati Corse racing team, overseeing their successful return to GT racing in the early 2000s.

In 2002, Steiner joined the newly-formed Red Bull Racing team as their sporting director. He played a key role in building the team from scratch, helping to recruit drivers and staff, and overseeing the team's first Formula One season in 2005.

After leaving Red Bull Racing in 2006, Steiner worked as a consultant for various motorsport organizations before joining the Haas F1 Team as team principal in 2014.

Under Steiner's leadership, the Haas F1 Team made their debut in the 2016 Formula One season and quickly established themselves as a competitive force in the sport. Steiner's focus on teamwork and collaboration played a key role in the team's success, and his experience and expertise proved invaluable in navigating the complex world of Formula One racing.

Overall, Guenther Steiner's career in motorsport has been characterized by a deep passion for the sport and a commitment to excellence. His experience as a rally driver and team manager, combined with his leadership skills and strategic vision, have made him a respected and influential figure in the world of motorsport. As the sport of Formula One continues to evolve and change, Steiner's expertise and experience will undoubtedly continue to be valuable assets in shaping the future of the sport.

Jaguar (2001–2003)

After retiring from competitive driving, Guenther Steiner began working for the Jaguar Racing team in 2001. He served as the operations director for the team, overseeing their logistics and operational planning.

Steiner's time at Jaguar was a challenging period for the team, as they struggled to achieve competitive success in Formula One. Despite the difficulties, Steiner remained committed to the team's goals and worked tirelessly to help them improve.

In 2003, Jaguar Racing was acquired by the Red Bull energy drinks company, and Steiner left the team to join the newly-formed Red Bull Racing team as their sporting director. His experience and expertise would prove invaluable in helping to build the team from scratch and establish them as a competitive force in Formula One racing.

Absolutely. After joining the newly-formed Red Bull Racing team in 2003, Guenther Steiner played a key role in building the team from the ground up. He was responsible for overseeing the team's sporting operations, including driver selection, race strategy, and team logistics.

Under Steiner's leadership, the Red Bull Racing team quickly established themselves as a competitive force in Formula One racing. They achieved their first podium finish in 2006, and their first race win in 2009.

Steiner's experience and expertise proved invaluable in navigating the complex world of Formula One racing, and his focus on teamwork and collaboration helped to foster a positive and supportive team culture at Red Bull Racing.

In 2006, Steiner left Red Bull Racing to work as a consultant for various motorsport organizations, including the FIA and the GP2 series. He also served as a team manager for the Maserati Corse racing team, helping to oversee their successful return to GT racing.

In 2014, Steiner joined the Haas F1 Team as team principal. Under his leadership, the team made their debut in the 2016 Formula One season and quickly established themselves as a competitive force in the sport.

Overall, Guenther Steiner's career in motorsport has been characterized by his deep passion for the sport, his commitment to excellence, and his focus on teamwork and collaboration. His experience and expertise have made him a respected and influential figure in the world of motorsport, and his contributions to the sport will undoubtedly continue to be felt for many years to come.

Certainly. As the team principal of the Haas F1 Team, Guenther Steiner has overseen the team's growth and development in the highly competitive world of Formula One racing.

Under Steiner's leadership, the Haas F1 Team has established a reputation for their innovative approach to racing, including their use of advanced simulation technology to optimize performance on the track.

Steiner's focus on teamwork and collaboration has also been a key factor in the team's success. He has fostered a positive and supportive team culture, encouraging open communication and constructive feedback among team members.

Despite the challenges of competing in Formula One racing, Steiner remains committed to the team's goals and is always looking for ways to improve and stay ahead of the competition. His strategic vision and deep understanding of the sport have made him a highly respected figure in the world of motorsport.

Overall, Guenther Steiner's career in motorsport has been defined by his passion, commitment, and expertise. His contributions to the sport as a rally driver, team manager, and racing executive have left a lasting impact on the world of motorsport, and his leadership at the Haas F1 Team continues to inspire and influence the next generation of motorsport professionals.

Red Bull (2005–2008)

Guenther Steiner was not the sporting director for Red Bull Racing during that time.

As you stated, after Red Bull purchased Jaguar Racing in 2004, Steiner was invited to join the team as the technical operations director in January 2005. Together with team principal Christian Horner, he helped lead the team to improved results in the 2005 season. However, when Red Bull Racing hired Adrian Newey as their technical director, Steiner was approached by team owner Dietrich Mateschitz to help establish a NASCAR team in the United States.

Feeling that the F1 team had become overcrowded, Steiner consulted with his wife and agreed to move to Mooresville, North Carolina, where he served as Team Red Bull's technical director from April 2006 to April 2008. During his time with the team, Steiner played a key role in establishing their presence in the NASCAR series, overseeing the development of their cars and working closely with drivers and engineers to optimize performance on the track.

Overall, Guenther Steiner's experience with Red Bull Racing and Team Red Bull helped to further hone his skills as a racing executive, and prepared him for the challenges and opportunities that awaited him in his future roles as a team manager and principal in Formula One.

Haas (2014)

After leaving his role at Team Red Bull in April 2008, Guenther Steiner returned to Europe and began consulting for various racing teams and organizations. In 2014, he was approached by Gene Haas, an American businessman and NASCAR team owner, about the possibility of starting a new Formula One team.

Steiner was immediately intrigued by the idea, and agreed to become the team principal for Haas F1 Team. Together with Haas and a small group of engineers and designers, Steiner began laying the groundwork for the new team, working tirelessly to secure the necessary funding, personnel, and resources to compete in Formula One.

The team faced a number of significant challenges in their early years, including the daunting task of building a car from scratch and competing against established teams with far greater resources and experience. However, Steiner's leadership and determination helped to keep the team focused and motivated, and their hard work paid off with a successful debut season in 2016, during which they finished eighth in the Constructors' Championship.

Since then, Haas F1 Team has continued to grow and evolve under Steiner's guidance, with a focus on developing young talent and leveraging innovative technologies to improve performance. Despite facing ongoing challenges in a highly competitive and rapidly changing sport, Steiner remains committed to building a successful and sustainable Formula One team for the long term.

Under Steiner's leadership, Haas F1 Team has continued to make steady progress in the Constructors' Championship, with the team finishing eighth in 2017 and fifth in 2018. However, the 2019 season proved to be a significant setback for the team, as they struggled to adapt to new technical regulations and fell to ninth place in the championship standings.

Despite this setback, Steiner remained committed to the team's long-term vision and continued to invest in new talent and technologies. In 2020, the team introduced a brand new car, the VF-20, and signed two promising young drivers, Romain Grosjean and Kevin Magnussen, to lead the team on track.

The season proved to be a challenging one for the team, with a number of setbacks and disappointing results. However, Steiner's leadership and determination helped to keep the team focused and motivated, and they were ultimately able to finish ninth in the championship standings.

Looking ahead, Steiner and Haas F1 Team remain committed to building a successful and sustainable Formula One team for the future, with a focus on developing young talent and leveraging innovative technologies to improve performance. Despite the ongoing challenges of the sport, Steiner's passion and dedication to racing continue to inspire and motivate his team, as they work to achieve their goals and realize their vision for the future of Formula One.

The 2021 season saw significant changes for Haas F1 Team, as the team opted to field an all-rookie driver lineup, consisting of Mick Schumacher and Nikita Mazepin. The team also announced that they would be focusing their resources on developing their 2022 car, in order to better compete under the new technical regulations.

Despite the challenges of fielding a young and inexperienced driver lineup, Steiner remained optimistic and committed to the team's long-term vision. He continued to work closely with the team's engineers and designers to develop the VF-21, and remained focused on building a sustainable and successful team for the future.

While the team faced significant struggles on track during the 2021 season, Steiner's leadership and determination helped to keep the team motivated and focused on their goals. He continued to invest in the team's infrastructure and personnel, and remained committed to developing the next generation of racing talent.

Looking ahead, Steiner and Haas F1 Team remain focused on the future, with a renewed focus on building a competitive and sustainable team under the new technical regulations. With Steiner at the helm, the team is well-positioned to continue making progress and achieving their goals in the years to come.

Personal life

Guenther Steiner is a private person and has not shared much about his personal life publicly. However, it is known that he is married and has children. He is fluent in multiple languages, including Italian, English, and German.

Steiner is known for his passion for racing and his dedication to his work. He has been described as a hard worker who is always focused on achieving his goals, and he is highly respected in the motorsports community for his expertise and leadership.

In his free time, Steiner enjoys sports and outdoor activities. He has also been involved in various charitable initiatives, supporting causes such as children's education and environmental conservation.

Printed in Great Britain
by Amazon

38496520R00020